Happy Mother's Day 84
Connie

Rodale's *High Health* Cookbook Series

LOW-COST
NATURAL
FOODS

Rodale's *High Health* *Cookbook Series*

LOW-COST
NATURAL
FOODS

by the Editors of Rodale Books

Series Editorial Director:
Charles Gerras

Text Preparation:
Carol Munson
Camille Cusumano

Recipe Research and Editing:
Camille Bucci

Illustrations:
Jean Gardner

Art Director:
Karen A. Schell

Series Designer:
Jerry O'Brien

Copy Editing:
Jan Barckley

Cover Photography:
Carl Doney

Food Stylist:
Laura Hendry Reifsnyder

Rodale Press, Emmaus, Pennsylvania

Printed in the United States of America on recycled paper, containing a high percentage of de-inked fiber.

The recipes in this book have appeared in other Rodale publications.

Library of Congress Cataloging in Publication Data
Main entry under title:

Low-cost natural foods.

(Rodale's high health cookbook series ; v. 1) Includes index.
1. Cookery (Natural foods) I. Rodale Books. II. Series.
TX741.L68   641.5'637   81-20991
ISBN 0-87857-390-9   hardcover   AACR2

2   4   6   8   10   9   7   5   3   1   hardcover

Contents

How You Can Eat Better and Spend Less

*E*very cuisine in the world offers a raft of delectable, wholesome favorites that are made from simple, low-cost ingredients. The Italians cook up countless varieties of filling pastas and combine them with a little cheese or meat, smothered with a flavorful sauce. In the Middle East, people blend bits of lamb with spices and bulgur to make the traditional, highly seasoned — and economical — entree called kibbi. Latin Americans savor chili — a thick, spicy stew of simmered tomatoes, beans, and, when they can afford it, meat. We Americans can learn a lot from these centuries-old traditions. A hearty and appetizing meal doesn't have to be expensive.

Imaginative cooks have countless opportunities for money-saving creativity, especially when they start with natural ingredients. Think of the choice of grains — not only wheat, rye, oats, and rice, but the less familiar millet, buckwheat, barley, bulgur, and cornmeal. And how about the countless varieties of beans, peas, and lentils, and all the bright vegetables available in the market! Add to these the endless combinations possible with nuts, seeds, herbs, spices, eggs, yogurt, cheese, and fruit. With all these at hand, why would anyone settle for the flat taste of costly frozen dinners, fast-food burgers, vegetables in a pouch, or frozen pizzas?

THE HIGH COST OF PROCESSING

It isn't hard to see why meals made with natural ingredients are more interesting and less expensive than those concocted from processed foods. When food processors do the work for you, they decide on the ingredients and how to blend the flavors in such dishes as casseroles, dressings, sauces, cakes, breads, and soups. That explains the "sameness" about these food products.

In a blind taste test conducted by the *New York Times,* nine people, including four school children, compared four dishes made from dinner mixes (such as Hamburger Helper or macaroni and cheese) and four homemade look-alike versions made from simple ingredients found in the average kitchen. In three of the four samples, all nine testers preferred the homemade dinners.

The manufacturers also charge for the work, the packaging, the advertising, and the transportation involved in getting the product to you. That explains the high prices for inferior foods. The final tally for turning foods into ready-to-eat or ready-to-heat wonders is often several times the cost of the food itself. Consider this: You pay nearly 300 times more for flavored gelatin than for plain, and commercially made yogurt costs more than 8 times what you spend to make yogurt at home.

The Cost of Processing

Minimally Processed Food	Highly Processed Food	Increase
Frozen Broccoli (10 ounces)	Frozen Broccoli with Butter Sauce (10 ounces)	52%
Frozen Spinach (10 ounces)	Frozen Creamed Spinach (10 ounces)	64%
Dried Kidney Beans (1 cup)	Canned Kidney Beans (1 cup)	127%
Potatoes (1 pound)	Potato Chips (1 pound)	721%

Highly processed foods cost more in terms of nutrition, too. When you stretch a meat loaf at home, you can do it with wheat germ and whole grains that are rich in B vitamins and high in fiber. You might boost the nutrient levels of breads, biscuits, and cream soups by blending in fruits, vegetables, and dried powders from milk. Processors, on the other hand, usually add modified food starches, cornstarch, and bleached flour—foods so refined that the nutrients are gone—to stretch and thicken

8

products. Worst of all, they generally flavor foods with liberal quantities of sodium, sugars, and saturated fats (for example, coconut oil and lard in snacks).

The Added Element

Peas, fresh, cooked (1 cup)	2 milligrams sodium
Peas, frozen (1 cup)	184 milligrams sodium
Peas, canned (1 cup)	588 milligrams sodium
Tomato Juice, homemade—no salt added (6 ounces)	7 milligrams sodium
Tomato Juice, commercial (6 ounces)	364 milligrams sodium
Apricots, fresh (2 whole)	12 grams carbohydrates
Apricots, canned (2 whole)	20 grams carbohydrates
Yogurt, Banana, homemade—no sugar or honey added (8 ounces)	12 grams carbohydrates
Yogurt, Banana, commercial (8 ounces)	49 grams carbohydrates

TAKE FULL ADVANTAGE OF FRESH FRUITS AND VEGETABLES

Serve generous quantities of low-priced fresh fruits and vegetables as a major step in extending your food budget. Both have plenty of fiber, especially when served raw, which makes them filling, and they are loaded with desirable nutrients.

Carrots, potatoes, turnips, and other root vegetables make excellent extenders for meat stews, hearty chowders, and poultry casseroles. If a menu includes side dishes of chilled applesauce, steaming peas and rice, and cauliflower with hot cheese sauce, only a small portion of meat is needed to create a most substantial meal.

Buy fresh fruits and vegetables in season for top quality, best taste, and lowest prices. Buy directly from a farmer who grows his own produce, if you can. When that is not convenient, shop in a market that keeps its produce cold and where the turnover is high. Since fruits and vegetables (and their nutrients) are perishable, buy them shortly before you plan to use them.

Look for fruits and vegetables that are without defects and are of moderate size—oversized or undersized ones are rarely a bargain. Fresh produce should have a bright color and should be ripe yet feel firm.

Good preparation techniques can make the difference between a great-looking, great-tasting fruit or vegetable and an inferior product. Wash produce thoroughly, but do not soak. (Exceptions are sandy spinach, cauliflower, broccoli, and cabbage with bugs. Soak those vegetables only enough to remove the unwanted extras.) While washing, inspect the produce for damaged spots you want to remove before cooking or serving.

Because exposure to light and air begins the destruction, cut fruits and vegetables just before you are ready to use them. (When you can avoid it, don't cut them at all.) To lessen bruising, slice firm fruits and vegetables with a sharp knife, but tear sensitive greens. When you cook fruits and vegetables, use a minimal amount of water and cook them for the shortest time possible.

Put your senses to work when you serve fruits and vegetables. Take advantage of their colors (deep reds, soft greens, bright oranges) and textures (crisp, smooth, grainy) to enhance the appeal of all your meals.

GETTING YOUR MONEY'S WORTH FROM MEAT

Since meat purchases—along with poultry and fish—account for the largest part of many food budgets, making the most of each purchase is essential in producing low-cost meals. One easy way to reduce expenditures for meat is to mix it with grains, beans, and other vegetables in casseroles, soups, and stews. Stretching meat loaves and patties with blends of whole grains, sprouts, whole-grain bread crumbs, cheeses, eggs, and wheat germ is a fine way to enhance flavor and is very practical, too.

The less tender cuts of meat are generally the least expensive, so why not extend your food budget even more by using these? With long slow cooking in moist heat, such cuts can be as tasty as the most costly ones. Use them in noodle casseroles, rich soups, stews, and as pot roasts. Or mince them, add tomatoes and spices, and turn them into a rich sauce for pasta or rice. Mixed with onions, other herbs, and a dressing, minced meat can be spread on crackers to make an appetizer so satisfying that meat won't be missed in the main course.

Braising and simmering are the ideal methods for preparing the less tender cuts of beef, lamb, and pork, including the organ meats. In either cooking method, subtle use of herbs, spices, fruits, and vegetables helps to bring out the full flavor of the meat.

To braise meat, brown it slowly on all sides in just enough fat to keep the meat from sticking to the pan. Then, add a small quantity of broth, juice, or water (½ cup or less) to prevent overbrowning. Cover the pan and cook the meat over low heat or in a 350°F oven until it is tender. Use a heavy pan with a tight-fitting lid, because the meat will cook for an hour or more, and it is important to retain every bit of moisture.

To simmer a roast or a smaller cut of meat, brown it first (if desired) on all sides in a small amount of fat. Pour in enough water, broth, or juice to cover the meat. Add herbs or spices and place a tight-fitting lid on the pot. Simmer (do not boil) the meat slowly over low heat until it is tender when pierced by a fork.

10 Popular Herbs and Where to Use Them

Basil	Sauces, casseroles, poultry, stuffings, soups
Chives	Vegetables, grains, sauces, eggs
Dill	Vegetables, fish, breads
Garlic	Meats, fish, poultry, pilafs, casseroles, sauces
Marjoram	Beans
Mint	Grains, vegetables
Oregano	Sauces, casseroles, soups
Parsley	Pilafs, casseroles, soups, breads
Tarragon	Beans, poultry
Thyme	Casseroles, beans, meats, poultry, fish

COOKING WITHOUT MEAT STRETCHES THE BUDGET EVEN MORE

Of course, meatless meals make optimum use of inexpensive natural foods. If your family usually eats a lot of meat, try serving one no-meat meal a week, then two or three, according to the response you get. At the same time, expand the variety of grains, nuts, seeds, legumes, and dairy products used in the entrees and side dishes at those meals to insure a wide range of tastes, textures, and nutrients.

USE MORE LEGUMES, GRAINS, AND NUTS

Legumes have been called "the meat that grows on vines" because of their high protein levels—20 to 40 percent! They are also fine sources of the B vitamins, calcium, iron, and fiber; they contain little fat, they are low in sodium, and they cost less than any other source of protein.

For optimum-quality dried beans, select those that are bright in color, clean, plump, and free from insect damage. They will keep for months when stored in a tightly covered container in a cool, dry place.

Cooking Dried Beans

- Sort through the beans and discard any damaged beans, tiny twigs, leaves, or stones.
- Soak the beans in cold water that's 3 to 4 times their volume for 6 to 8 hours, or boil them (also in 3 to 4 times the water) for 2 minutes and then let them soak in the hot water for 1 hour.
- Cook the soaked beans in gently simmering water or in a pressure cooker (follow the manufacturer's directions for use) for the length of time given in the chart.

Bean	Time in Simmering Water	Time in Pressure Cooker
Adzuki	45–50 minutes	15–20 minutes
Black Turtle	45–60 minutes	10 minutes
Black-eyed Pea	60 minutes	10 minutes
Chick-pea (garbanzo)	2 hours	15–20 minutes
Fava	45–60 minutes	not recommended
Lentil	30 minutes	6–8 minutes
Lima	45–60 minutes	not recommended
Baby Lima	45–60 minutes	not recommended
Mung	1½ hours	8–10 minutes
Pinto	1½ hours	10 minutes
Red Kidney	1½ hours	10 minutes
Small White Bean	45–60 minutes	4–5 minutes
Soybean	3 hours	15 minutes
Split Pea	35–40 minutes	not recommended

- Use the beans in a favorite soup or casserole recipe or try a new one from this book.
- Store unused, cooked beans in the refrigerator or freezer.

Note: Eating legumes sometimes results in flatulence. To lessen its effects, discard the soaking water and cook the beans in fresh water. After 30 minutes of cooking, discard that water and finish the cooking in another potful of fresh water. The process does lose some nutrients, but it also rids the beans of the gas problem.

You can use cooked beans to add body and nourishment to salads, soups, stuffed peppers, cabbage rolls, and rice dishes. Puree legumes to make thick and substantial dips, spreads, sauces, and dressings. Try all kinds of legumes in your cooking, since each type can make its own unique contribution to a dish.

Among the legumes, the soybean reigns supreme in terms of nutritional value, with a 30 to 40 percent protein content that closely resembles the amino acid pattern of animal protein. Though its popularity is just dawning in the Western countries, the Chinese and the Japanese have recognized its worth for centuries and have used it to create a wide variety of food products.

Tofu, the best-known soy product, is pulpy and custardlike, and it is an ideal food for those cutting back on meat. It can be sauteed for adding to soups, sandwiches, salads, or main dishes; whipped as the base for mayonnaise, dips, or salad dressings; crumbled for blending with meat in meatballs; even cubed for making bread pudding. Served in quantities of one to three ounces per person, tofu is a bargain protein. It's available in the produce section of many large supermarkets and most natural foods stores. It is made by innoculating cooked soybeans with a special culture and then incubating them for 24 hours.

Tempeh is a fragrant, firm, chewy white cake with a mild, meaty flavor and is especially rich in vitamin B_{12}. Tempeh can be fried, baked, broiled, or simmered. It works well as a burger, a tempura, in a casserole, or added to a soup.

Hearty, whole grains are right up there with beans when it comes to providing outstanding plant protein. Wheat and oats, for example, are almost 15 percent protein. And, if you combine them with nuts, seeds, legumes, or—best of all—dairy products, the protein quality is improved dramatically.

Shop for grains that still have the bran and germ intact. Whole grains provide the best nutrition. Store them in the refrigerator or the freezer so that the oil in the germ does not turn rancid.

You can serve grains in a number of appealing ways, but breads— flat, quick, and yeast—are probably the most popular. Yet, grains are also exceptionally tasty and satisfying when simply simmered in water or broth and topped with chopped nuts. Sauteed for a pilaf, grains take on a nutlike flavor and chewy texture that make it difficult to stop with one helping. For breakfast, cooked porridges provide creamy warmth and sustenance on cold winter mornings.

Pastas made with whole grains, and spinach, beets, or carrots, retain

Cooking Grains

Regular Method

- Rinse grains in cold water *only* if they seem gritty. Grains contain B vitamins, which are readily washed away.
- Measure the amount of cooking liquid (it can be water, broth, or juice) suggested in the chart and bring the liquid to a full boil in a large pot.
- Add the grains to the boiling liquid and stir once.
- Return the liquid to a boil, then lower the heat. Cover the pot and slowly cook the grains until they are soft and the liquid has been absorbed.
- Use the taste test to determine if the grains are done. They should be somewhat chewy, neither tough nor hard.

Grain (1 cup)	Liquid (cups)	Cooking Time	Yield (cups)
Barley	3	1¼ hours	3
Buckwheat Groats	2–5	15 minutes	2½
Cornmeal	4	25 minutes	3
Millet	3	45 minutes	3½
Oats	3	30–40 minutes	3½
Rice (Brown)	2	45 minutes	3
Wheat	3	2 hours	2⅔
Cracked Wheat	2	25 minutes	2⅓
Bulgur Wheat	2	15–20 minutes	2½

- Keep cooked grains in the refrigerator or freezer.

Pilaf Method

- Saute 1 cup of the grain with 1 medium onion (and 1 clove garlic, 1 sprig parsley, or ½ cup mushrooms) in oil.
- Add the liquid—approximately twice as much liquid as grain—and cover the pan.
- Cook the grain over low heat until the liquid is absorbed and the grain is tender.

all the goodness of those foods and are another wholesome addition to low-cost, natural meals.

With the wide array of shapes and sizes of pasta available, it is easy to see why it is welcome at any meal. Macaroni, smothered with hot cheese sauce and baked until a golden brown crust forms, evokes fond childhood memories of Saturday lunch. To impress special guests, you can sauce and stuff shells, ravioli, or manicotti for a filling, yet scrumptious, elegant main dish. As a side dish, lightly buttered noodles garnished with poppy or sesame seeds lend a pleasant, simple touch to an elaborate dinner. You can even take a chilled macaroni-and-chicken salad to a picnic instead of fried chicken.

Cooking Pasta

- Bring a minimum of 3 quarts of water to a full, rapid boil in a large, covered pot.
- Add 1 tablespoon of oil (it will prevent the cooked pasta from sticking together); then gradually pour in the macaroni, spaghetti, or noodles. To fit long strands of spaghetti into the pot, break the strands in half, or place one end in the boiling water and, as the spaghetti softens, coil the strands around the pot until all are completely underwater.
- Cook the pasta, uncovered, until it is tender yet slightly chewy (8 to 10 minutes for small macaroni and noodles; longer for manicotti and lasagna). Test for doneness by tasting a piece or by pressing it with a fork against the side of the pot or biting through a strand. When done, it should break cleanly and easily.
- Drain the pasta in a colander; do not rinse.
- Serve the pasta immediately with a bubbling hot sauce, mix it with prepared casserole ingredients, or toss it with salad fixings.

Nuts and seeds are often overlooked as a major souce of plant protein for meatless meals. Peanuts (which are actually legumes) are the best source, with 26 percent protein; walnuts and pistachios have about 20 percent; others have slightly less. A nutritional profile shows that besides protein, each nut and seed contains fiber, vitamins B and E, and several minerals. Use nuts to boost the protein quality, flavor, and crunch of a dish whenever you can.

When buying whole nuts in the shell, choose those that have no cracks, stains, or holes. Watch out for moldy nuts; they are dangerous to eat. In shelled nuts, pick those that are plump, firm, and light in color.

Nuts in their shells keep well at room temperature for a short time. To retain maximum freshness over a long period, store them in a cool, dry place. Shelled nuts should be refrigerated in tightly closed containers. All nuts maintain excellent quality in the freezer.

You can put nuts and seeds to work in limitless ways. Sliced, ground, chopped, or whole, they perk up ordinary batters and doughs, pilafs and stews, salads and sauces. They are an unexpected, happy surprise when folded into a souffle. Granolas and breakfast cereals have added appeal with chopped cashews, almonds, or pumpkin seeds. Sprinkle ground almonds, walnuts, or sesame seeds over steamed green beans or sliced chilled tomatoes to give a new dimension to familiar standbys.

Once you start cooking with low-cost natural foods and savor the robust flavors they offer, you'll wonder why you waited so long to enjoy them!

APPETIZERS, SNACKS, AND CEREALS

LOW-COST APPETIZERS

The dishes of nibbles a hungry crowd goes through as they socialize or as they watch television can easily break the bank. People who buy boxes of crackers, jars of spreads, or boxes of commercial breakfast cereals know how fast these extras can swallow up a chunk of the budget. If cutting food costs is a need, this is one of the first places to apply the scalpel: You can either stop serving these foods, *or* cut costs by making your own.

Some of the dips you buy in the store can be duplicated at home with little more effort than it takes to open the supermarket package. More important, you have control — no chemicals, no coloring, more garlic, less pepper, no salt. Have it your way.

Do you object to the airy puffs of cereal that cost dollars for ounces of color and crunch? Make your own and save the dollars while you pump up your family's health with tasty cereals rich in nutrients.

You'll be surprised at how easy and enjoyable it is to make your own crackers, your own relishes, your own anything the stores sell as a snack food. You don't have to stop eating appetizers and snacks to save, just stop *buying* them.

1 tablespoon oil

1 small onion, coarsely chopped

1 clove garlic, coarsely chopped

¼ teaspoon savory

¼ teaspoon thyme

½ pound chicken livers

1 hard-cooked egg

pepper to taste

Herbed Liver Spread

*P*lace oil in a small skillet. Saute onion, garlic, savory, and thyme until onion is transparent.

Add livers and cook over medium heat until just done. Remove skillet from the heat and allow livers to cool for a few minutes. Blend by dropping through the opening in blender top 1 liver at a time, with motor going at high speed.

Blend in egg and pepper to taste.

Yields 1 cup

*W*hen peeling a hard-cooked egg, start at the large end. If the shell is stubborn—an egg 3 or 4 days old usually peels more easily than a fresher one—peel it off under cold running water.

Lima Bean and Sesame Dip

½ cup sesame seeds

1 10-ounce package frozen lima beans, cooked

¼ cup coarsely chopped onions

¼ cup mayonnaise

¼ cup yogurt

1 to 2 teaspoons lemon juice

*T*oast sesame seeds in a dry heavy skillet over medium heat, stirring constantly to prevent scorching, just until their aroma becomes apparent. Grind toasted sesame seeds to a meal in a blender.

Combine cooked lima beans with onions and puree in blender until smooth, using a little of the cooking liquid if necessary.

Turn out into a medium-size bowl, add sesame meal and remaining ingredients, and stir until well combined.

Yields about 2 cups

1 tablespoon milk

1 small onion, quartered

¼ pound Cheddar cheese, cut
into ½-inch chunks

Onion-Cheese Spread

*M*easure milk into a blender. Turn the machine on to medium speed and drop onion quarters, one at a time, through the opening in blender top.

Blend cheese similarly. Help cheese onto the blades with your spatula, with motor off.

Let set overnight to allow flavors to blend.

Yields about ½ cup

*I*f peeling an onion makes you cry, keep back those tears by skinning the onion under cold running water. Some cooks say holding a piece of bread between your teeth checks the tears too.

Radish, Carrot, and Apricot Relish

¼ cup vinegar

1 tablespoon honey

⅔ cup shredded radishes, red or white

¼ cup shredded carrots

3 dried apricots, cut in strips

*I*n a small saucepan, combine vinegar and honey and bring to a boil.

Combine remaining ingredients in a medium-size bowl and pour vinegar-honey mixture over all. Cover and let marinate in refrigerator at least 30 minutes.

Yields about 1 cup

*T*o simplify cutting dried apricots and other dried fruits, use scissors dipped in oil (to prevent sticking) instead of a knife. If the cut fruit is destined for a cake or bread, lightly dust the fruit with flour before cutting. (Use a portion of the flour called for in the recipe.)

1 cup cornmeal

1 cup whole wheat flour

½ cup water

2 tablespoons oil

3 ounces sharp Cheddar
cheese

Cornmeal-Cheese Crackers

*P*reheat oven to 300°F.

Combine dry ingredients in a medium-size bowl.

Combine water, oil, and cheese in container of an electric blender, process until smooth, and stir into dry ingredients, making a stiff dough.

Roll out dough on an oiled baking sheet to ⅛-inch thickness. Score with knife and bake 20 minutes. If desired, top with grated cheese and cumin seeds and toast under broiler to melt cheese before serving.

Makes about 4 dozen crackers, each 2 inches square

1 pound sunflower seeds

3 tablespoons oil

¼ teaspoon cayenne pepper

3 tablespoons tamari soy
  sauce

½ teaspoon celery seed,
  ground

¼ teaspoon paprika

Sunflower Seed Snack

*P*reheat oven to 350°F.

In a shallow baking pan, combine sunflower seeds with other ingredients. Mix together and bake 20 minutes, stirring after 10 minutes.

Remove pan from oven and drain sunflower seeds on paper towels to remove excess oil.

Cool and store in tightly covered container.

Yields about 2 cups

Note: If recipe is doubled, be sure to bake a little longer (30 to 35 minutes).

*R*oasting nuts or seeds is the perfect activity for a chilly autumn afternoon. Mix 1 teaspoon of oil with each cup of shelled nuts or seeds for a rich flavor and even browning. Spread them on a baking sheet and bake, stirring occasionally, at 350°F until they are lightly browned (5 to 12 minutes).

3 cups oatmeal

1 cup any other flaked or rolled grain

1 cup bran

2 cups any combination of nuts and seeds

1 cup coconut, grated

½ cup soy grits (optional)

brewer's yeast to taste (optional)

nonfat dry milk to taste (optional)

Cooked Bran Granola

¼ to ½ cup honey

¼ cup oil

½ cup water

vanilla to taste (optional)

1 to 2 cups chopped raisins or dried fruit (optional)

*P*reheat oven to 250°F.

In a large bowl, combine all dry ingredients except raisins or dried fruit. Combine honey, oil, water, and vanilla, if desired, in a separate small bowl and add gradually to dry ingredients, stirring to coat grains and nuts evenly.

Bake in a lightly oiled baking pan 1 to 1½ hours, stirring every 15 minutes until granola is dry and lightly browned and crisp. Remove from oven, add fruit, if desired, cool, and store in airtight container.

Yields 8 to 12 cups

Sesame-Rice Cereal

¾ cup brown rice, uncooked

1 cup skim milk powder

3½ cups water

2 tablespoons sesame seed meal (sesame seeds briefly ground in blender)

1 tablespoon nutritional yeast

*T*oast rice in a medium-size dry skillet over medium heat, stirring until well browned. Grind in a blender, then toast the powder again briefly, in dry skillet, stirring constantly.

Combine skim milk powder and water with a wire whisk. Put in a heavy saucepan and bring to a boil. Add rice powder, stirring constantly.

Lower heat and simmer, covered, about 10 minutes, or until cereal is thick. Toast sesame meal in dry skillet over medium heat, stirring constantly for a minute or so, and add to cereal. Stir in nutritional yeast and serve with milk and honey.

Serves 4 to 6

SOUPS

LOW-COST SOUPS

Soup surely inspired the phrase, "a lot from a little!" Consider how easily one can turn the picked-clean carcass of a chicken or turkey into a potful of fragrant, nutritious goodness. Think how soup can transform bruised or leftover vegetables and a little rice into a hearty, satisfying dish. Soup has been the salvation of many a cook when funds were running low.

The first thing a soup-maker learns is *Never Throw Anything Away.* All kinds of leftovers can perform second duty as the base for a stock (meat, fish, or poultry bones particularly); or as hearty fillers — vegetables from the previous night's dinner, grains that billowed into more than the family could consume at one meal, a chunk of roast that nobody claimed. What seemed to be a nearly total loss reappears as a fantastic contribution to the table!

Even when you set out to make soup with specially purchased ingredients, you can create a dish everyone will greedily devour, yet you need spend very little money. A thick, hearty pea soup, a burly lentil and barley soup, a warming, filling corn chowder — any of these will fill up the hungriest family, while using ingredients that certainly qualify as economical.

Remember this: In Europe the custom of starting a meal with soup arose from the hope that guests or family would fill up on this inexpensive course, permitting the thrifty hostess to serve small portions of the costlier entree. It's an idea that still serves well in an emergency.

Black Bean Soup

1 cup black beans

1 medium-size onion, coarsely chopped

1 green pepper, coarsely chopped

1 stalk celery, coarsely chopped

1 carrot, coarsely chopped

2 cloves garlic, finely chopped

3 tablespoons oil

2 cups chicken stock

lemon juice to taste

snipped chives

*I*n a 3-quart pot, soak beans overnight in enough cold water to cover. Drain, add fresh water to cover, and then simmer until they are almost tender (about 2 hours).

In a large skillet, cook all the chopped vegetables in oil until they are almost tender and then add to the beans. Add chicken stock and simmer until beans are tender. Remove from heat and allow to cool slightly. When cool, puree in an electric blender. Return to pot, add lemon juice, heat, and serve with snipped chives.

Serves 6 to 8

6 ears of corn

2 medium-size onions, coarsely
    chopped

3 small potatoes, cubed

2 tablespoons butter

½ teaspoon paprika

1 teaspoon kelp powder

⅛ teaspoon pepper

⅓ cup water

3 cups milk

1 teaspoon honey

2 bay leaves

Corn Chowder

With a sharp knife, make a deep cut down the center of each row of kernels. Cut the kernels off the cobs into a large bowl. Scrape the cobs to get all the corn pulp and milk into the bowl.

In a large heavy pot or Dutch oven, lightly saute onions and potatoes in butter until lightly browned (about 10 minutes). Add paprika, kelp, pepper, and water, cover, and simmer 8 minutes.

Add corn, milk, honey, and bay leaves. Simmer gently 20 minutes. Remove bay leaves.

Serves 4

2 cups diced celery

2 tablespoons oil

½ medium-size onion, coarsely chopped

4 cups chicken or turkey stock

¾ cup skim milk powder

¾ cup water

½ teaspoon kelp powder

chopped parsley for garnish

Cream of Celery Soup

*I*n a small skillet, saute celery in oil until almost tender. Remove ½ cup of celery and set aside—to add to the soup at the end.

Then add onions to the pan and continue to saute until they and the celery are tender.

Puree sauteed celery and onions to desired consistency for the base of your soup. Pour puree into top of a double boiler and start it heating. Add stock.

In a small bowl, combine skim milk powder and water (with a wire whisk, not blender) and add it near the end, just giving it time to heat sufficiently for serving.

Add reserved celery and kelp. Garnish with parsley.

Yields about 6 cups

*D*ried milk solids added to sauces and cream soups increase protein and calcium. You can use 3 tablespoons of milk solids with each cup of liquid.

1 to 2 cloves garlic

1 medium-size onion, sliced

1 cucumber, sliced

3 tomatoes, peeled

1 green pepper, coarsely chopped

4 eggs

   cayenne pepper to taste

¼ cup vinegar

¼ cup olive oil

¾ cup tomato juice

Gazpacho

Garnish

1 cucumber, diced

1 bunch green onions, diced

1 green pepper, finely chopped

Process the first 5 vegetables and eggs in an electric blender, or put vegetables through a food grinder and mix with beaten eggs. Add cayenne and liquids and chill.

To garnish, add diced vegetables to soup just before serving.

Serves 6

Always peel garlic, unless otherwise directed. The thin, translucent skin comes off easily if you first slightly crush the clove with the flat of the blade of a wide-bladed knife.

German Lentil Soup

1 pound lentils (3 cups)

2 quarts cold water

1 beef bone

2 medium-size onions, diced

2 carrots, diced

½ cup diced celery

1 medium-size potato, peeled and grated

2 bay leaves

¼ teaspoon dried thyme

½ teaspoon pepper (optional)

2 teaspoons lemon juice

Put lentils into a large soup pot with cold water. Add beef bone, vegetables, bay leaves, thyme, and pepper, if desired.

Place over medium heat and bring gently to a boil. Lower heat and simmer until lentils and vegetables are soft.

Remove beef bone and bay leaves from soup. Skim excess fat from soup. Remove meat from beef bone, dice, and add to soup.

Slowly stir in lemon juice and serve immediately.

Yields about 8 cups

½ cup minced onions

2 tablespoons oil

3 cups chicken stock

3 cups pumpkin puree

nutmeg to taste

toasted whole-grain croutons
for garnish

Pumpkin Soup

*I*n a small skillet, saute onions in oil until golden but not brown. Put in a blender container with a little of the chicken stock and blend until pureed.

Combine onion mixture, remaining stock, and pumpkin puree in a heavy-bottom saucepan. Heat, add nutmeg to taste, and serve with toasted croutons.

Yields about 6 cups

*F*or an ultrasmooth pumpkin puree, put cooked, mashed pumpkin through a food mill or a sieve. Hubbard or any other winter squash can be used as an excellent substitute when pumpkin is not available.

Vichyssoise (French Potato Soup)

3 medium-size leeks, sliced

1 medium-size onion, sliced

2 tablespoons oil

4 medium-size potatoes, peeled and sliced fine

4 cups chicken stock

1 cup skim milk powder

1 cup water

chopped chives or parsley for garnish

*I*n a large skillet, saute leeks and onion in oil until soft. Add potatoes and chicken stock and simmer, covered, until vegetables are very tender. Lift vegetables out of stock and put them through a food mill. Then return to pot with stock.

Combine skim milk powder and water with a wire whisk and add to pureed soup. Return soup to low heat. Serve either hot or chilled, garnished with chopped chives or parsley.

Yields about 6 cups

MAIN DISHES

LOW-COST MAIN DISHES

If meat, poultry, and fish account for a major part of the money your family spends on food, you are indeed keeping up with the Joneses — and most other families. Maybe those folks don't have to concern themselves about saving money on these items, but if you do, the recipes in this section will help you to accomplish your goal.

Some dishes make the most of a little meat to add savor to a large dish full of other good things. For example, favorites such as stuffed cabbage rolls or Turkey Tetrazzini have so much other goodness going on in them that the little bit of meat it takes to fill out and balance them seems like plenty.

You will see that dishes calling for larger portions of meat emphasize inexpensive cuts or low-cost organ meats. Hash and chili will work with the toughest (therefore the least expensive) cuts of meat; chicken livers are versatile, nutritious, and usually a good bargain.

Finally, main dishes that require no meat at all are champion money-savers that offer tremendous variety. Egg dishes, such as quiches and omelets, or casseroles that feature tofu or cheeses are ideal.

A steak or a roast is the least imaginative way to tackle the main course in a menu plan. Make the most of less costly, more interesting alternatives.

Almond, Vegetable, and Tofu Saute

1 cup water

2 teaspoons cornstarch

2 tablespoons tamari soy sauce

2 teaspoons chicken stock or vegetable soup base

¼ teaspoon garlic powder, or 1 clove garlic, crushed

1 cup thinly sliced carrots

1 cup cut green beans

2 tablespoons oil

1 cup sliced cauliflower

1 medium-size onion, sliced

1 cup cubed tofu

½ cup slivered roasted almonds

*I*n a small bowl, combine water, cornstarch, tamari, stock, and garlic. Set aside.

In a wok or large skillet, stir-fry carrots and beans in oil over fairly high heat 2 minutes. Add cauliflower and onion and stir 1 or 2 minutes longer. Then add sauce mixture and cook until thickened. The vegetables will be crisp. If you like them softer, cover and cook a bit longer.

Add tofu and cook just until warmed. Sprinkle almonds over the dish before serving. Serve immediately with brown rice. For variety, top with roasted peanuts—this changes the flavor considerably.

Serves 4 to 6

A Pound of Unshelled Nuts Equals—		
Nut	Shelled Weight (ounces)	Shelled Volume (cups)
Almonds, whole	6⅓	1¼
Coconut, shredded	8⅓	3
Peanuts, roasted	11⅔	2⅓
Pecans, halves	8½	2¼
Walnuts, Black, chopped	3½	¾
Walnuts, English, halves	7¼	2

1 cup bulgur

1 medium-size onion, minced

2 green peppers, finely chopped

1 cup chopped walnuts

2 tablespoons olive oil

2 tablespoons safflower oil

1 tomato, cut carefully into
    ½-inch pieces

1 teaspoon dried oregano

2 pounds whole fish (bass,
    bluefish, mackerel, etc.)

½ cup tahini

2 cloves garlic

3 to 4 tablespoons lemon juice

1 to 1½ cups water

Garnish

  sliced lemons

  chopped parsley

Baked Fish
with Walnut-Bulgur Stuffing and Garlic-Sesame Sauce

*P*reheat oven to 350°F.

Soak bulgur in enough water to cover about 5 minutes. Drain and reserve excess water for soup. Saute onion, peppers, and walnuts in oils a few minutes. Add drained bulgur and tomato, stirring to combine.

Stuff fish, cover with foil, and bake 20 to 30 minutes, or until fish is tender.

Put tahini in a blender container. Add garlic, salt, lemon juice, and just enough water to blend to a smooth puree. Serve warm or cold, but if heating it, be careful to use low heat and to stir constantly to prevent lumping and scorching.

Glaze fish with garlic-sesame sauce and serve topped with lemon slices and parsley.

Serves 4 to 6

1½ cups cooked brown rice

3 eggs

¼ cup skim milk powder

1 cup water

dash of freshly ground pepper

dash of nutmeg

1 tablespoon potato flour or brown rice flour

1¼ cups shredded sharp Cheddar cheese (or part natural Swiss and part Cheddar)

Cheese Quiche
in Brown Rice Shell

*P*reheat oven to 375°F.

Press cooked rice into an oiled 9-inch pie plate. Bake just until dry (about 5 minutes); cool.

In a medium-size bowl, beat eggs until light and fluffy. Combine skim milk powder and water with a wire whisk and add to eggs, along with pepper and nutmeg.

Add flour to cheese; toss lightly but thoroughly. Put into cooled rice shell, spreading to edges of crust. Pour egg-milk mixture over all and bake 10 minutes. Reduce heat to 325°F and continue to bake 25 to 30 minutes longer, or until filling puffs up and is golden brown.

Remove from oven; allow to set about 5 minutes; cut into wedges and serve.

Serves 6

*E*ggs are generally available in 4 sizes: small, medium, large, and extra large. To get the most egg for your money, buy the larger size when there is less than a 10 percent difference in price between 2 sizes.

1 pound ground beef

2 medium-size onions, coarsely
      chopped

1 cup coarsely chopped celery

½ cup coarsely chopped green
      peppers, including the
      seeds

1 clove garlic, minced

1 tablespoon oil

2 cups coarsely chopped
      tomatoes

1 cup tomato puree

½ cup catsup

1 teaspoon cumin

1 tablespoon chili powder

  dash of cayenne pepper

2 cups cooked kidney beans
      (or any cooked beans)

Chili Con Carne

Saute beef, onions, celery, green peppers, and garlic in oil, using a heavy skillet. Stir in tomatoes, tomato puree, and catsup. Add seasonings, cover, and simmer about 30 minutes.

Add beans, adjust seasoning, and continue to simmer 10 to 15 minutes longer. Serve on brown rice or in whole wheat pita pockets.

Serves 6

Chinese Chicken Livers

2 tablespoons tamari soy sauce

1 tablespoon cornstarch

1 teaspoon honey

1 pound chicken livers

¼ cup oil

1 slice ginger root, finely chopped

2 large cloves garlic, minced

1 cup snow peas

½ cup chopped bamboo shoots

1 cup sliced water chestnuts

4 large mushrooms, sliced

2 tablespoons lemon juice

slivered almonds for garnish

In a small bowl, combine tamari, cornstarch, and honey to make a paste.

In a wok or heavy skillet, saute chicken livers in oil about 5 minutes. Remove chicken livers and set aside. Saute ginger and garlic in same pan until golden brown. Then add snow peas, bamboo shoots, water chestnuts, and mushrooms. Cook 4 minutes, stirring constantly.

Stir in lemon juice and the paste mixture. Then add livers and cook over medium heat until sauce thickens. Serve over brown rice and garnish with slivered almonds.

Serves 4

6 eggs

4 green onions, thinly sliced

¾ cup frozen green peas

1 cup chopped mushrooms

1½ cups mung bean sprouts

1 tablespoon tamari soy sauce

2 tablespoons oil

Egg Foo Yung

*I*n a large bowl, beat eggs. Add remaining ingredients, except oil, combining well.

Heat oil in a skillet to a medium-high temperature. Ladle 2 tablespoons of the mixture into skillet for each pancake. When pancakes are set and brown underneath, turn them over and brown the other side. Serve immediately.

Serves 4 to 6

*S*oybean sprouts are delicious when sauteed or simmered 6 to 8 minutes and added to salads, casseroles, soups, or breads. To make full use of the nutrients in soybean sprouts, always cook them before eating.

3 tablespoons oil

1 rump or chuck roast
   weighing 4 to 5 pounds

3 medium-size onions,
   coarsely chopped

¼ teaspoon ground cloves

Fruited Pot Roast

2 cups apple juice or apple
   cider

1½ cups dried prunes

1½ cups dried apricots

2 to 4 tablespoons cornstarch

¼ cup cold water

*I*n a heavy-bottom pot, heat oil to medium-high temperature. Brown meat on all sides.

Add onions, cloves, and apple juice or cider and cover tightly. Lower heat and simmer 2 hours, or until nearly tender.

Add prunes and apricots and continue to cook 30 minutes longer.

If desired, thicken liquid in pot with cornstarch dissolved in cold water.

Serves 10

Note: Roast can also be cooked in a 350°F oven. After browning meat, transfer to a roasting pan with close-fitting lid. Add onions, cloves, and liquid. Cover tightly and cook 2½ hours. Then add prunes and apricots, and cook 30 minutes longer.

*W*hen buying meat, stay alert for bargains in all price categories. To find the most economical cut, calculate the price per serving. Occasionally, an expensive cut (high price per pound) is the best buy because the waste from bone, fat, and gristle is minimal. Little waste keeps the price per serving low.

4 to 6 green or red peppers,
   uncooked

2 cups cooked brown rice

1 large carrot, shredded

¼ cup uncooked peas

1 stalk celery, finely chopped

½ cup finely chopped uncooked
   cauliflower

2 scallions, thinly sliced

2 hard-cooked eggs, chopped

Garden-Style Stuffed Peppers

Dressing:

2 tablespoons oil

2 tablespoons vinegar

1 tablespoon lemon juice

1 teaspoon dry mustard

Slice tops off peppers and remove seeds and membranes. Dice tops and combine with rice, remaining vegetables, and eggs in a large bowl.

In a small bowl, combine dressing ingredients and pour over rice mixture. Chill at least 1 hour to blend flavors.

Pack stuffing into peppers and serve immediately or chill until needed. The cold rice mixture can be stored in the refrigerator for a day if necessary.

Serves 4 to 6

Garden Sukiyaki

1 cup sliced turnips or parsnips

2 cups sliced zucchini or other summer squash

½ cup sliced leeks

1 cup sliced cauliflower

2 cups sugar peas

1 cup sliced carrots

3 cups sliced beet greens or other greens

2 pounds round steak, pork, or boned chicken

3 tablespoons tamari soy sauce

1 tablespoon honey

3 tablespoons cornstarch

3 tablespoons oil

½ pound tofu, diced

1 pound mung bean or lentil sprouts

Slice all vegetables into uniform strips, about 2 inches long and 1 inch wide and ⅛ inch thick; cut parsnips, zucchini, and carrots lengthwise. Keep each variety separate. Sugar peas and sprouts can be left whole. Greens can be chopped in 2-inch squares.

If meat is partially frozen, it is easier to slice. Cut into pieces about the same size as the vegetables.

Combine tamari, honey, and cornstarch and set aside.

Garden Sukiyaki—continued

Heat a wok, Dutch oven, or very large skillet to medium-hot. Add the oil and saute the meat, stirring often. When almost done, add turnips or parsnips, squash, leeks, cauliflower, and carrots, stirring to coat vegetables with oil and meat juices.

Cover and cook briefly until vegetables are barely tender. Check and stir often, as it doesn't take long to cook these small pieces.

Add peas, greens, and tofu and cook until greens get a bit wilted. Stir often. Then add the sprouts and pour tamari into the juices in the pan (just move aside the vegetables a bit). Cook and stir until the sauce thickens (about a minute).

Serve immediately.

Serves 8

Note: The variety of this dish is as endless as the things you like to eat. Green beans, shredded cabbage, and broccoli are just some of the other vegetables that can be used in this dish.

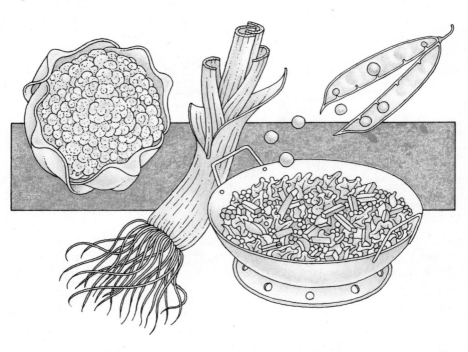

Halupkis
or Cabbage Rolls

1 large head cabbage, enough
to yield 12 good-size
cabbage leaves

1 small onion, minced

1 clove garlic, minced

1½ tablespoons oil

1½ pounds ground beef

1 egg, beaten

1 cup cooked brown rice

¼ teaspoon summer savory

¼ teaspoon pepper

¼ cup wheat germ

3 tablespoons nutritional
yeast (optional)

Sauce:

4 teaspoons potato flour or
brown rice flour

2 cups tomato juice

4 tablespoons catsup

*P*reheat oven to 325°F.

With a sharp knife, cut core from head of cabbage. Parboil in boiling water about 8 to 10 minutes. Remove and allow to cool before handling. Then remove a few leaves at a time and trim away thick ridge on back of leaf, to make it easier to roll.

Halupkis—continued

In a small skillet, saute minced onion and garlic in oil.

In a large bowl, mix ground beef, egg, rice, and sauteed onion and garlic. Add pepper, wheat germ, and nutritional yeast, if desired.

Spread each leaf (on thick end) with meat mixture, fold the two sides over and roll, starting with the thick end. Fasten with toothpicks, if necessary. Place rolls in an oiled baking pan.

Using a small saucepan, slowly add flour to tomato juice, stirring constantly with wire whisk or wooden spoon. Then add catsup. Cook over low heat until thickened, stirring constantly, and pour over cabbage rolls.

Cover pan and bake 1 hour. Then remove cover and bake another 20 minutes, or until the rolls are tender and lightly browned.

Serves 6

Note: 1 pound of leftover, cooked, ground meat may be substituted for 1½ pounds raw meat.

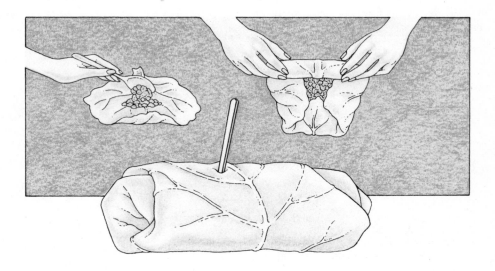

1 cup dried corn

1 cup water

1 calf heart (approximately 1 pound)

1 tablespoon wheat germ

1 tablespoon rye flour

2 tablespoons oil

1 cup chopped onions

½ teaspoon dried basil

½ teaspoon dried thyme

3 tablespoons chopped parsley

⅛ teaspoon pepper

Hearty Hash

Grind dried corn as fine as possible in a food mill or electric blender. Add water and set aside to soak about 30 minutes.

Meanwhile, trim off fat and any arteries from the heart and cut into ½-inch cubes. Dust with wheat germ and flour. Saute in oil, turning to brown all sides, about 5 minutes.

Add onions and continue to saute until tender. Then add soaked corn (with water), herbs, and pepper. Saute 5 minutes longer and serve.

Serves 4 to 6

Note: Kidney or liver may be substituted for the heart, or a combination of all three.

2 tablespoons oil

1 2½-pound broiler-fryer, cut up,
     or 2½ pounds chicken legs

1 pound sweet potatoes, peeled
     and cut into 1½-inch slices

1 cup unsweetened pineapple
     juice

⅓ cup minced celery leaves

1 bay leaf, crumbled

1 large green or red pepper (or
     combination of both), sliced

1 medium-size onion, sliced,
     or 8 pearl onions

2 cups fresh peas or frozen peas,
     thawed

Skillet Chicken Dinner

*H*eat oil in a large skillet and brown chicken on all sides; spoon off fat. Add sweet potatoes, pineapple juice, celery leaves, and bay leaf. Simmer, covered, 20 minutes, or until chicken and sweet potatoes are tender. Add green or red pepper, onions, and peas and cook until tender-crisp.

Serves 4

Stir-Fried Kidneys

1½ tablespoons tamari soy sauce

1½ tablespoons lemon juice

2 teaspoons cornstarch

2 pounds veal, pork, or lamb kidneys

2 tablespoons oil

4 green onions, including tops, sliced into 1-inch pieces

1 tablespoon sesame seeds

Combine tamari, lemon juice, and cornstarch. Prepare kidneys using basic method (see below), then cut into slices. Place them in tamari–cornstarch mixture, cover, and refrigerate 1 to 2 hours, stirring occasionally.

Heat oil in a heavy skillet or wok until medium hot. Pour in kidney mixture and stir-fry 1 minute. Add onions and sesame seeds and continue to stir-fry about 5 minutes longer, or until pinkness of kidneys is completely gone. Serve immediately.

Serves 3 to 4

Basic Method for Preparing Kidneys

Before washing kidneys, snip out the white tissue from the center with kitchen scissors. Then wash in water or in a vinegar and water solution if preferred. This will help to remove any strong odor during cooking. Drain. Cut the kidneys into cubes as small or as large as desired. Cook according to recipe but take care to avoid cooking kidneys too long or at too high a temperature. Heat toughens them and causes them to give off a strong odor during cooking.

1½ cups tomato sauce

2 teaspoons tamari soy sauce

4 teaspoons water

12 pieces of tempeh, 2½ inches each

¼ cup whole wheat flour

1 egg, beaten with 1 tablespoon water

1 cup fine whole-grain bread crumbs

¼ cup olive oil

½ pound mozzarella cheese, thinly sliced or grated

¼ cup grated Parmesan cheese

Tempeh Parmesan

Spread a thin layer of sauce over the bottom of an oiled 10-inch-square ovenproof casserole. Reserve remaining sauce.

Combine the tamari and water and mix well.

Dip each piece of tempeh into the water-tamari mixture, then into the flour to coat evenly. Dip each piece into the egg, then into the bread crumbs, shaking off the excess.

Brown the slices in a thin layer of olive oil in a heavy skillet and place them in the casserole. Spread mozzarella cheese over the top evenly, cover with the remaining tomato sauce, and sprinkle with the Parmesan cheese.

Bake at 400°F until cheese melts (about 15 minutes).

Serves 4

Turkey Tetrazzini

½ pound whole wheat noodles
   or spaghetti

3 quarts boiling water

1 tablespoon oil

¼ pound mushrooms, sliced

4 tablespoons butter

¼ cup light cream

½ cup grated Parmesan cheese

2 cups cubed, cooked turkey

*C*ook noodles or spaghetti in 3 quarts boiling water to which 1 tablespoon oil has been added. Drain and rinse with cold water.

Preheat oven to 375°F. Saute mushrooms in 1 tablespoon butter 5 minutes. Meanwhile, to the cooked noodles or spaghetti, add remaining butter, cream, and grated cheese (reserving 2 tablespoons of cheese for top of casserole). Toss gently until thoroughly mixed, then place half the mixture in a buttered ovenproof casserole. Place the turkey on this and cover with mushrooms and the remaining pasta. Top with the 2 tablespoons of cheese. Bake 20 to 25 minutes, or until nicely browned.

Serves 6

*B*e careful not to overcook pasta. Shorten the cooking time slightly if pasta is to be used in a casserole or soup that requires further cooking.

1 cup wheat berries

3 cups water

4 medium-size potatoes

1 pound ground beef

1 onion, finely chopped

5 tablespoons oil

⅓ cup whole wheat flour

2 teaspoons chopped parsley

½ teaspoon dried sweet basil

Wheat Berry and Beef Casserole

*I*n a 2-quart saucepan with a very tight fitting lid, combine wheat berries and water. Bring to a boil, cover, and remove from heat. Wrap pot in newspapers or a heavy woolen blanket and allow to stand overnight in a warm place. Drain and reserve liquid.

Cook and mash potatoes.

Saute beef and onion in 2 tablespoons oil, drain, discard excess fat, and set mixture aside. Heat remaining 3 tablespoons oil in a skillet, stir in flour, and cook for a minute or so. Then add 1½ cups reserved wheat berry liquid and cook, stirring constantly, until mixture is thick and smooth. Add herbs.

Preheat oven to 350°F. Butter a 2½-quart ovenproof casserole and put wheat berries in the bottom, then a layer of meat covered with half of the sauce. Top casserole with mashed potatoes and pour remaining sauce over them. Bake about 30 minutes, or until casserole is hot and bubbling.

Serves 8

Wheat-Soybean Casserole

½ cup soybeans

1 cup wheat berries

2 cups corn, fresh or frozen

2 cups cooked tomatoes, drained

1 cup coarsely chopped onions

1 clove garlic, crushed

½ teaspoon dried thyme

pinch of cayenne pepper

¼ cup tomato paste

3 tablespoons brewer's yeast (optional)

½ cup chicken, beef, or vegetable stock

⅓ cup grated cheese

Cook soybeans and wheat berries according to preferred methods. Drain and reserve liquid for soup or gravy.

In a large bowl, combine cooked soybeans, corn, tomatoes, onions, garlic, thyme, and cayenne. Set aside.

Preheat oven to 350°F. Combine tomato paste, brewer's yeast, if desired, and stock. Set aside.

Place half the cooked wheat berries on the bottom of an oiled 4-quart ovenproof casserole. Cover this layer with the soybean mixture. Spread the tomato paste mixture over the soybean layer and top casserole with remainder of wheat berries. Sprinkle with grated cheese. Bake, uncovered, 30 minutes.

Serves 6 to 8

3 medium-size zucchini

¼ cup olive oil

1 pound lean ground beef

1 onion, coarsely chopped

3 eggs

1 tablespoon chopped parsley

⅛ teaspoon garlic powder

2 cups milk

2 tablespoons cornstarch

1 cup shredded mild Cheddar
   cheese

Zucchini Moussaka

*P*reheat oven to 350°F.

Slice zucchini crosswise. In a large skillet, lightly brown zucchini slices in oil. Remove from pan and set aside.

In the same skillet, brown beef and onion. Drain off fat and allow beef to cool. Beat together eggs, parsley, and garlic powder and combine with beef.

Heat 1¾ cups milk in a medium-size saucepan. Dissolve cornstarch in remaining ¼ cup cold milk. Add cornstarch mixture to hot milk, stirring constantly, and cook until mixture thickens and bubbles. Add cheese and cook, stirring, until it is just dissolved.

Layer zucchini, meat, and sauce in a 2-quart ovenproof casserole, beginning and ending with sauce. Bake 30 minutes.

Serves 4

SIDE DISHES

LOW-COST SIDE DISHES

Many cooks make their biggest money-saving moves with the side dishes they serve. Diners are so taken with one or two supporting dishes, they don't even notice that the hamburger patties are less plump than usual, or that the chicken breast is divided into four pieces instead of two. And that's the idea!

A wise cook can build up quite a repertoire of these valuable distractions and thereby save herself considerable main-course money. Anyone can take advantage of these helpers.

One way is to keep a mental file of your family's favorite vegetables and grains. Come up with some unusual versions of these favorites that you know will tempt them every time. Then present a heaping dish of one or two when those foods are in season and your bank balance is sagging. The family will be so busy wolfing down the specialties that the rest of the meal will seem incidental.

Another useful approach is to serve an interesting grain dish, such as the bulgur-squash combination included in this section, or the Green Bean Casserole with Corn Bread Topping. Such dishes are appealing, nutritious, and truly do provide an answer to the problem of feeding a family well with limited funds.

1 medium-size onion, coarsely
  chopped

¼ cup sunflower oil

4 cups cooked navy beans (1½
  cups dry)

1 cup reserved bean broth or
  vegetable broth

⅓ cup tomato paste

2 tablespoons maple syrup

1 tablespoon cider vinegar

1 teaspoon dry mustard

 pinch of freshly grated nutmeg

¼ cup corn germ

All-American Beans

*P*reheat oven to 300°F.

Saute onion in 3 tablespoons of oil until soft. Mix with beans. Add bean broth, tomato paste, maple syrup, vinegar, and spices and mix well.

Place in a 1-quart ovenproof casserole. Sprinkle top with corn germ and dribble the remaining tablespoon oil over all.

Bake 1 hour, until top is crunchy and brown.

Serves 6

Breaded Veggies

3 cups sliced zucchini, eggplant, cauliflower, Jerusalem artichokes or other vegetables, about ¼ inch thick

2 eggs

¼ cup milk

corn germ

*P*resteam "hard" vegetables, such as cauliflower or broccoli.

Mix egg and milk in a small bowl. Dip vegetables into egg mixture, then into corn germ, coating thoroughly. Let stand 5 minutes before sauteing in a large skillet over moderate heat until veggies are tender and breading is crisp but not overbrowned.

Oven method: Drizzle breaded veggies with melted butter or oil. Bake at 350°F until crisp.

Serves 6

4 cups boiling water

2 cups bulgur

1 teaspoon paprika

2 cups yogurt

¼ cup sesame oil

1 egg, beaten

¼ cup chopped chives or green
onions

5 cups cubed summer squash

⅓ cup grated cheese

⅓ cup toasted sesame seeds

whole wheat bread crumbs

butter

Bulgur-Squash Casserole

*P*our boiling water over bulgur and let stand until water is absorbed. Stir paprika into bulgur.

Preheat oven to 350°F. Combine yogurt, sesame oil, egg, and chives or green onions.

Spread bulgur in a 7 × 11-inch baking pan. Arrange squash over bulgur and sprinkle grated cheese over squash. Pour yogurt sauce over mixture, top with bread crumbs and toasted sesame seeds, and dot with butter.

Bake until squash is tender.

Serves 10 to 12

*Y*ogurt sometimes separates, or curdles, when heated. To help stabilize it for cooking, blend 1 slightly beaten egg white and 1 tablespoon of flour (or cornstarch or arrowroot) with 1 quart of yogurt. Slowly bring the mixture to a boil, stirring continuously in one direction. Reduce the heat and gently simmer, uncovered, 10 minutes. Cool and refrigerate until needed.

Chard-Egg Loaf

2 carrots, grated

1 medium-size onion, minced

1 tablespoon oil

2 cups cooked chopped chard

6 eggs, beaten

½ teaspoon dried oregano

½ teaspoon dried thyme

Preheat oven to 350°F.

In a large skillet, saute carrots and onion in oil until tender. Add chard.

Stir eggs into vegetables, add seasonings, and mix well.

Pour into greased loaf pan, dot with butter, and bake 40 to 45 minutes, or until eggs are set.

Serves 8

2 cups frozen corn
(about ⅔ package)

1 cup boiling water
(approximately)

2 tablespoons butter

2 tablespoons rye flour

1 cup water

¼ cup skim milk powder

¼ cup finely chopped green
peppers (optional)

2 egg yolks

¼ teaspoon paprika

2 egg whites

Corn Pudding

*P*reheat oven to 350°F.

Cook corn in boiling water until tender. In a blender, process corn and liquid together briefly to mash it, but not long enough to puree it.

In a large saucepan, melt butter and stir in flour gradually until blended. In a small bowl, combine water and skim milk powder with a wire whisk and add gradually, cooking over low heat until sauce is thickened. Add corn mixture and then add green peppers, if desired.

In a small bowl, beat egg yolks. Add a small amount of the corn mixture to the yolks, stirring constantly, and then return to the remaining corn mixture. Stir and cook over low heat several minutes to allow egg yolks to thicken slightly. Add paprika.

Beat egg whites until stiff, but not dry, and fold them lightly into the corn mixture. Turn into a 1½- to 2-quart ovenproof casserole and bake 30 minutes.

Serves 4 to 6

Eggplant and Tomatoes

1 small onion, coarsely chopped

2 tablespoons oil

1 medium-size eggplant, cubed

2 large or 3 small tomatoes, coarsely chopped

dash of pepper

1 teaspoon dried oregano

several leaves basil, minced

1 tablespoon chopped parsley

*I*n a medium-size saucepan, brown onion in oil. Then add eggplant, tomatoes, and seasonings. Cover and simmer about 30 minutes, or until vegetables are tender.

Serves 4

*T*ake full advantage of vine-ripened tomatoes during the summer. They are inexpensive and have twice the vitamin C of those grown in greenhouses during the winter.

1½ pounds fresh green beans, trimmed

1¾ cups milk

2 tablespoons butter

dash of white pepper

2 tablespoons whole wheat flour

Corn Bread:

1 cup cornmeal

½ cup whole wheat flour

3 teaspoons baking powder

1 egg

⅔ cup milk

2 tablespoons honey

3 tablespoons butter, melted and cooled

Green Bean Casserole
with
Corn Bread Topping

*P*reheat oven to 400°F.

Cook beans until tender-crisp. Drain, reserving liquid. Place beans in a buttered 9-inch-square baking dish. Pour bean liquid into a 2-cup measure and add enough milk to make 2 cups.

In a small saucepan, heat 1½ cups of the milk with butter and pepper. Pour remaining ½ cup milk into a jar. Add flour to the jar, cover, and shake until smooth. Pour flour mixture into scalded milk, stirring constantly, and cook until the sauce bubbles and thickens. Pour over beans.

In a medium-size bowl, mix dry ingredients for the cornbread with a fork until well blended. In another saucepan, beat together egg, milk, honey, and melted butter. Pour all at once into dry ingredients. Stir until just mixed. Spoon batter over beans and sauce. Bake 20 to 25 minutes, or until corn bread is risen and brown on top.

Serves 6 to 8

Italian-Style Snap Beans

1 pound snap beans

2 to 3 tablespoons oil

1 clove garlic, sliced

⅓ to ½ cup grated Parmesan
   or mozzarella cheese

¼ cup chopped parsley

Wash beans, snap off the ends, and break into 1-inch pieces. Steam beans until *almost* tender, about 5 minutes. Drain well.

Heat oil in a large skillet, and lightly saute the garlic a few minutes. Add beans and cook until tender, about 5 to 10 minutes, stirring often.

Season with cheese and parsley. Mix together well and serve piping hot.

Serves 4 to 6

Parmesan and mozzarella are two cheeses that are virtually synonymous with Italian cuisine. Yet, they are totally different in taste and texture. Parmesan is a hard, granular cheese with a sharp, piquant flavor. It's excellent grated over pasta or greens. Mozzarella, a semisoft, elastic cheese, has a delicate flavor. Because it shreds nicely and melts quickly, mozzarella is the perfect cheese for making pizza or veal parmigiana.

2 cups cooked brown rice

1 cup grated Cheddar cheese

4 eggs, beaten

2 tablespoons chopped parsley

⅛ teaspoon pepper

1 pound kale

1 tablespoon oil

2 tablespoons wheat germ

2 tablespoons soft whole-grain
    bread crumbs

Kale and Brown Rice

*P*reheat oven to 350°F.

Combine cooked rice, cheese, and eggs. Add parsley and pepper.

Wash kale, strip off leaves, and steam until almost tender.

In an oiled ovenproof casserole, arrange alternate layers of rice and kale, ending with rice.

Combine oil, wheat germ, and crumbs. Top casserole with bread crumb mixture and bake 30 minutes.

Serves 6

*B*uy cheese in bulk for shredding or grating if you want to save money and get full flavor and aroma. The supermarket shakers cost considerably more and deliver considerably less in quality.

  When working with shredded or grated cheese that's called for in a specific amount, pile it very gently into the measuring cup. One-half pound of cheese yields about 2 cups when shredded or grated.

Mashed Rutabaga

1¾ pounds rutabagas, peeled

1 tablespoon butter

¼ cup milk

dash of nutmeg or ½ teaspoon chopped mint

Dice rutabagas and steam 15 to 20 minutes, or until tender.

Drain and add butter and enough milk to make a smooth consistency.

Mash like potatoes, sprinkle with nutmeg or mint, and serve immediately.

1 cup mung beans

1 cup uncooked brown rice

2½ cups water

½ cup finely chopped or thinly sliced onions

½ cup chopped green peppers

3 tablespoons oil

2½ cups chopped tomatoes

2 teaspoons tamari soy sauce

⅛ teaspoon cayenne pepper

¼ teaspoon crushed basil

Mung Beans and Rice

Wash mung beans, cover with water, and soak overnight in refrigerator, or 5 to 6 hours at room temperature.

Pour beans and liquid used for soaking into a medium-size saucepan and bring to a boil. Simmer until tender (about 40 minutes). Drain beans and reserve liquid.

While mung beans are cooking, prepare brown rice. In another medium-size saucepan, bring 2½ cups of water to a boil. Add rice, cover, and simmer until rice is tender (about 40 minutes), stirring occasionally to prevent sticking. Remove rice from burner and drain any remaining liquid; set aside.

In a large skillet, saute onions and green peppers in oil until tender, but not brown. Add drained mung beans and rice. Stir in tomatoes and seasonings, along with ½ cup reserved liquid from beans and rice. Cover and continue to simmer mixture, adding more liquid if necessary, until flavors have blended (about 15 minutes).

Serves 8 to 10

Parsnips and Peas

1 onion, coarsely chopped

2 teaspoons sesame oil

1 pound parsnips, sliced

1 pound fresh black-eyed peas
   (2 cups shelled)

Saute onion in oil until clear (about 5 minutes). Add parsnips and peas and simmer over low heat about 30 minutes, or until tender.

Serves 4 to 6

2 tablespoons olive oil

3 cups grated red cabbage

1 cup mung bean sprouts

1 tablespoon caraway seeds
    (optional)

  tamari soy sauce to taste

1 tablespoon vinegar

Sauteed Red Cabbage and Sprouts

*H*eat oil in a cast-iron skillet. Saute cabbage 3 to 5 minutes.

Add sprouts and saute 2 more minutes.

Add caraway seeds, if desired, tamari, and vinegar and allow to cook gently as you toss together a few more minutes. Serve piping hot.

Serves 6

*A*dd a tablespoon of vinegar or lemon juice to red cabbage during cooking to help the cabbage stay red. The old German custom of cooking a tart apple with red cabbage has the same effect. If you forget to put the acid in during cooking and the cabbage turns purple, adding some later reverses the color change.

Turnips with Hot Lemon Dressing

1 pound yellow turnips or
    rutabagas

2 tablespoons butter or oil

½ tablespoon lemon juice

1 tablespoon chopped parsley

Cut turnips into 1- to 2-inch pieces. Steam until tender (15 to 20 minutes).

Heat butter or oil, lemon juice, and parsley 1 minute. Pour over hot turnips in serving dish.

Serves 4

Rutabagas are often waxed to keep them from losing moisture. They must be pared before cooking to remove the waxy coating.

½ cup walnuts

2 to 3 tablespoons oil

1 cup thinly sliced celery

1 cup thinly sliced onions

1 sweet red pepper, cut into
    thin strips (optional)

2 cups bean sprouts, rinsed

½ pound spinach, well washed

Sauce:

3 tablespoons tamari soy
    sauce

½ cup chicken broth or water

  pinch of ginger

⅛ teaspoon garlic powder

2 teaspoons cornstarch

1 tablespoon honey

Vegetables Oriental

*P*lace the walnuts in a small saucepan with enough water to cover. Bring to a boil. Drain.

In a large skillet, heat 1 tablespoon oil and stir-fry celery, onions, and red pepper, if desired, until tender-crisp. Remove with a slotted spoon. Then saute walnuts until light brown. Add more oil to the pan as needed. Remove walnuts and then stir-fry sprouts and spinach until spinach has just wilted. Return celery, onions, red pepper, and walnuts to the skillet.

In a small saucepan, combine all the sauce ingredients except the honey. Bring to a boil, stirring constantly. Then add honey and stir until dissolved. Pour sauce over vegetables, heat through, and serve.

Serves 4 to 6

Wheat Germ-Giblet Stuffing

1 cup brown rice

4 chicken livers

2 to 4 tablespoons butter

1 onion, coarsely chopped

½ cup coarsely chopped celery

1 cup wheat germ

½ cup chopped parsley

⅛ teaspoon pepper

½ to ¾ cup chicken stock

Cook rice according to preferred method (see Index).

Meanwhile, in a large skillet, saute chicken livers in butter. Remove them from skillet and chop coarsely. Using same skillet, saute onion and celery, using more butter if needed.

Combine cooked rice, chicken livers, wheat germ, and sauteed mixture. Add parsley, pepper, and ½ cup stock. Mix well, adding more stock if needed.

Yields 3½ cups

Wheat germ is the nutritional heart of wheat and is rich in protein, B vitamins, vitamin E, potassium, and zinc. Wheat germ should be kept in a tightly covered container in the refrigerator or, if not used regularly, in the freezer. Toasted wheat germ has slightly less food value but a longer storage time.

SALADS AND DRESSINGS

LOW-COST SALADS

Salads can be the perfect answer to budget blues. Some of the heartiest, most delicious, most impressive and nutritious dishes you can imagine come under the heading of salads. Best of all, it's no trick to keep the costs way down. Stretch your meat or fish leftovers by dicing or flaking them or making them into julienne strips that blend beautifully with vegetables in season and greens from the garden. All together they make a welcome main course, a fresh combination of textures and flavors. Set it all off with a dressing of your own making (store-bought dressings are an inferior and expensive product), and you really have something substantial for practically no cash outlay.

Not every salad is a leafy one. Salads made from cold, cooked whole grains, such as rice and bulgur, or cold beans and legumes are a rage these days. These inexpensive, nutritious foods are easily enhanced with mint, garlic or other herbs, nuts, seeds, bits of meat, or chopped vegetables to make a low-cost, appetizing one-dish meal. Don't forget the delectable possibilities a fruit salad presents. Use the fruits in season—always a bargain—as a base, with rich greens; or try some unexpected mixes such as onions, radishes, nuts, and seeds.

Let your impulses reign when it comes to salads. You can't go wrong!

Apple, Beet, and Tuna Salad

4 beets

1 7-ounce can water-packed tuna, drained

1 tart apple, cored and cubed

1 stalk celery, chopped

3 to 4 tablespoons mayonnaise

2 tablespoons lemon juice

1 tablespoon minced onions

¼ teaspoon dried dillweed

Cook beets in enough water to cover until tender. Drain, peel, and cube.

Combine all ingredients in a medium-size bowl. Chill. Serve on salad greens, topped with more mayonnaise, if desired.

Serves 4

Red beets have a rich royal color. To preserve that color and prevent it from leaching into the water as they cook, leave their skins on and 2 inches of their stems intact. Adding a little vinegar or lemon juice to the cooking water also helps preserve their bright color.

1 cup diced cooked beets

2 cups diced cooked potatoes

1 cup cooked green beans or peas

2 tart apples, cored and diced

3 tablespoons oil

3 tablespoons cider vinegar

lettuce leaves

mayonnaise

2 hard-cooked eggs, sliced

Dutch Vegetable Salad

*I*n a medium-size bowl, combine beets, potatoes, beans or peas, apples, oil, and vinegar. Toss gently to mix. Spoon the mixture onto a bed of lettuce on a platter. Cover with a thin layer of mayonnaise. Garnish with egg slices.

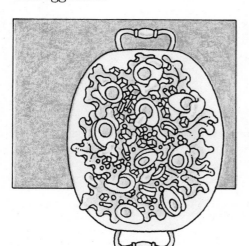

Serves 4 to 6

Golden Salad

2 tablespoons unflavored gelatin

⅓ cup cold water

1 cup hot unsweetened pineapple juice

⅓ cup honey

¾ cup orange juice

¼ cup lemon juice

1 cup coarsely grated carrot

1 cup cut-up orange segments

1½ cups drained unsweetened,
  crushed pineapple

Garnish

lettuce

mint leaves

orange sections

Soften gelatin in water and then dissolve mixture in hot pineapple juice. Stir in honey and blend well. Add orange juice and lemon juice. Cool mixture.

When mixture begins to thicken, fold in other ingredients.

Transfer gelatin mixture to a mold and chill until firm. Unmold on iceberg or romaine lettuce. Garnish and serve plain or with yogurt.

Serves about 6

Note: ⅔ cup chopped pecans or walnuts or 1 cup sliced bananas may be used in place of (or in addition to) orange segments.

⅓ cup cider vinegar

⅓ cup olive oil

3 tablespoons chopped parsley

1 teaspoon honey

¼ teaspoon crushed oregano

¼ teaspoon kelp powder (optional)

¼ teaspoon freshly ground pepper

⅓ cup sliced scallions, including
tender green tops

2 cups cooked garbanzo beans
(chick-peas)

2 cups cooked kidney beans

romaine or iceberg lettuce
leaves for garnish

Marinated Kidney Beans and Garbanzos

*T*o prepare marinade, combine vinegar, oil, parsley, honey, seasonings, and scallions. Blend together thoroughly.

In a medium-size bowl, combine garbanzo and kidney beans. Pour marinade over beans and toss lightly but thoroughly.

Place in refrigerator, covered, and marinate several hours or overnight, stirring occasionally.

Serve in bowl lined with outer leaves of iceberg or romaine lettuce.

Serves 8 to 10

*K*elp powder, made from seaweed, is high in sodium, but it's also rich in potassium, iodine, calcium, iron, and zinc.

Snappy Tossed Salad

1 cup chopped beet greens

1 cup chopped mustard greens

½ cup minced onions

⅓ cup mayonnaise

2 hard-cooked eggs, sliced

Stir together the greens and onions. Toss with mayonnaise and garnish with eggs.

Serves 2

Dark green leafy vegetables are richer in vitamin A, calcium, and iron than light green leafy vegetables.

½ cup coarsely ground bulgur

⅓ cup finely chopped onions

½ cup chopped parsley

3 tomatoes, chopped

⅓ cup lemon juice

1 teaspoon kelp powder

¼ cup olive oil

2 tablespoons finely chopped
     mint or 1 tablespoon dried-
     crumbled mint

Tomato- Bulgur Salad

Garnish

romaine lettuce

mint or parsley

*P*lace bulgur in a bowl and pour enough cold water over bulgur to cover completely. Allow it to soak about 10 to 15 minutes.

Drain bulgur in a sieve or colander lined with a double thickness of dampened cheesecloth. Wrap the bulgur in the cheesecloth and squeeze it vigorously until completely dry.

Place drained bulgur in a deep bowl and add onions, parsley, tomatoes, lemon juice, and kelp. Toss mixture gently but thoroughly. Place in refrigerator, covered, about 1 hour to blend flavors.

Just before serving, stir in olive oil and mint. Mound the salad in a serving dish surrounded by romaine lettuce leaves. Garnish with additional mint or parsley, if desired.

Serves 4 to 6

Vegetable Mold

2 cups diced tomatoes

1 envelope unflavored gelatin

3 tablespoons honey

2 teaspoons lemon juice

½ teaspoon grated lemon rind

½ cup diced celery

¾ cup shredded carrots

lettuce leaves for garnish

*P*lace tomatoes in a small saucepan. Sprinkle gelatin over tomatoes and mix together with a wooden spoon.

Place saucepan over medium heat and bring mixture to a boil. Remove from heat and add honey. Cool mixture. Stir in lemon juice and rind.

Add vegetables to tomato-gelatin mixture. Turn into a 1-quart mold and place in refrigerator 3 to 4 hours, or overnight, to set.

Unmold salad on serving plate lined with romaine or iceberg lettuce leaves. Serve with yogurt or cottage cheese.

Serves 4 to 5

2 cups whole wheat macaroni

1 tablespoon oil

1 pound fresh green beans, cut into 1-inch pieces (about 2 cups)

2 cups diced carrots

2 tablespoons chopped parsley

½ cup chopped green onions

½ teaspoon dried dillweed

½ teaspoon dried basil

½ teaspoon pepper

1 cup cottage cheese

1 cup ricotta cheese

2 teaspoons prepared mustard

2 tablespoons lemon juice

Whole Wheat Macaroni Salad
with Cheese Dressing

Cook macaroni in plenty of boiling water to which 1 tablespoon oil has been added. Drain and rinse with cold water. Cook green beans and carrots according to preferred method. Drain if necessary.

Combine macaroni, beans, carrots, and seasonings. Process cottage cheese and ricotta in an electric blender. Add mustard and lemon juice and blend until smooth. Toss macaroni mixture with cheese dressing until well coated. Chill and serve.

Serves 6

When using pasta in cold salads, add the dressing before the pasta cools. This blends the flavors more thoroughly and prevents sticking.

Basic Mayonnaise

2 egg yolks

2 tablespoons lemon juice

1 teaspoon honey

1 cup oil

*H*ave all ingredients at room temperature.

In a small mixing bowl, with electric beater set at medium speed, beat egg yolks, 1 tablespoon lemon juice, and honey. Add ¼ cup oil, 1 drop at a time, beating constantly.

Slowly add remaining oil, a tablespoon at a time in the beginning, beating well after each addition, then adding oil in a steady stream, beating continuously until mixture reaches a thick consistency.

Gradually add remaining 1 tablespoon lemon juice and continue beating until thoroughly combined.

Refrigerate, covered, in a glass container until ready to use. Mayonnaise will thicken during refrigeration.

Yields about 1 cup

1 cup yogurt

2½ cups mayonnaise

2 tablespoons lemon juice

¾ cup thinly sliced green
onions (including tops)

Green Onion Dressing

Combine yogurt and mayonnaise with a wire whisk. Add lemon juice and onions.

Store in glass, quart container in refrigerator, covered.

Yields about 4 cups

Yogurt, which is tangy and tasty, yet rich in B vitamins, protein, and calcium, is easily and inexpensively prepared at home. To make: heat 1 quart of reconstituted dry milk to just under boiling in a stainless steel or enameled saucepan. Cool to lukewarm and stir in about 2 tablespoons of plain store-bought yogurt (make sure it contains active cultures and no preservatives). Cover the pan and place it in a warm spot (an oven heated by a light or a sunny window). Allow the milk to rest until it thickens into yogurt (4 to 8 hours). Do not disturb the pan, for the yogurt may not set. Chill before serving. Yogurt keeps well in the refrigerator for 5 days.

Herb French Dressing

½ teaspoon dried summer savory

½ teaspoon dried rosemary

½ teaspoon dried chives or basil

½ cup oil

2 tablespoons wine vinegar

2 tablespoons cider vinegar

¼ teaspoon dry mustard

Crush herbs by mortar and pestle or by rolling with a rolling pin.

Put all ingredients together in bowl and whisk.

Store in a covered glass container in refrigerator.

Yields ¾ cup

BREADS

LOW-COST BREAD

In most of the world's cultures, bread is a basic element in every meal. Some of the reasons: Just about anybody can afford bread; it is loaded with nutrients; bread is delicious; and it is filling. Of course, all of the above apply specifically to the homemade, whole-grain product. Imagine Ivan and Natasha trying to get through a winter in Siberia on the kind of puffy white slices sold in our supermarkets! They would demand more substance and more flavor. Why should you settle for less?

You can save a lot of money and provide a lot of satisfaction for yourself and your family by baking your own bread. The investment is minimal and the return in terms of good eating cannot be matched.

Serve a thick slab of home-baked bread with a bowl of thick soup for lunch, and even a football player will leave the table satisfied. After school, give the kids a slice of Herb and Onion Bread or an Oatmeal-Banana Muffin slathered with butter as a snack, and watch them clamor for more. And think of the dollars you'll save on pizza for the gang when you make it yourself!

Herb and Onion Bread

5 teaspoons dry yeast

½ cup lukewarm water

½ cup chopped onions

3 tablespoons oil

½ cup nonfat dry milk

1¾ cups water

1½ tablespoons honey

½ cup chopped parsley

2 teaspoons dried dillweed

1 teaspoon dried oregano

¾ cup cornmeal

3½ to 4 cups whole wheat flour

Soften yeast in ½ cup lukewarm water. Cook onions in oil until golden.

Combine milk and water. Add onion mixture, honey, and herbs. Stir in yeast mixture. Beat in cornmeal. Beat in approximately 2 cups whole wheat flour. Stir in remaining flour by hand to make moderately soft dough. Turn out on lightly floured surface. Knead 3 to 5 minutes. Place in oiled bowl, turning once to oil surface. Cover bowl with clean towel and let rise in warm, draft-free place until doubled in bulk (about 1 hour).

Punch down dough. Divide in half. Place in 2 well-greased 1-pound coffee cans. Cover and let rise until doubled (30 to 45 minutes). Preheat oven to 350°F and bake 45 minutes, covering loosely with foil the last 15 minutes. Remove immediately from cans and cool loaves.

Makes 2 loaves

½ cup softened butter or oil

2 eggs

1 cup mashed bananas (2 or 3
   medium-size bananas)

½ cup honey

¼ cup yogurt

1 teaspoon baking soda

1½ cups whole wheat pastry flour

1 cup rolled oats

Oatmeal-Banana Muffins

*P*reheat oven to 375°F and butter 18 muffin cups.

In a mixer bowl, combine butter or oil, eggs, bananas, and honey. Mix together yogurt and baking soda and add to first mixture. Cream well.

Add flour to creamed mixture, mixing until just blended. Stir in oats.

Fill muffin cups two-thirds full of batter. Bake 18 to 20 minutes. Remove from pans and cool on wire rack.

Makes 18 muffins

*T*o boost the protein level of breads, muffins, cakes, and biscuits, substitute 2 tablespoons from every cup of wheat flour with soy flour and reduce the oven temperature by 25°F. Soy flour browns at a lower temperature than wheat flour.

Pizza

Dough:

2 tablespoons dry yeast

1¼ cups lukewarm water

1 teaspoon honey

1 cup soy flour, sifted

1 tablespoon nutritional yeast

2 cups rye flour

¼ cup oil

cornmeal to dust pans

Tomato Sauce:

1 cup chopped onions

3 cloves garlic, minced

2 green peppers, diced

2 tablespoons olive oil

2 tablespoons oil (sesame or safflower)

4 cups cooked tomatoes

¾ cup tomato paste

1 tablespoon dried oregano

1 tablespoon dried basil

2 teaspoons honey

2 cups grated mozzarella cheese (about 1 pound)

½ cup grated Parmesan cheese

Pizza — continued

Sprinkle dry yeast over surface of lukewarm water. Add 1 teaspoon honey. Let soak 5 minutes.

Combine soy flour, nutritional yeast, and rye flour. Add along with oil to dissolved yeast mixture. Turn out onto lightly floured surface and knead until dough is smooth and elastic. Place in an oiled bowl, cover with a damp cloth, and let rise 1 to 2 hours in a warm place until doubled. Stir down and knead once more, briefly.

Divide into 4 balls and roll each one out ⅛ inch thick on a baking sheet or pizza pan that has been dusted with cornmeal. Make a rim around the pizza by pinching the crust into an edge. It can be either round and cut into wedges or oblong, cut into squares.

Preheat oven to 450°F. In a heavy-bottom pot, saute onions, garlic, and peppers in mixed oils until tender. Add tomatoes, tomato paste, and herbs and simmer over low heat for 30 minutes or so until flavors are well blended.

Top each pizza with about 1 cup tomato sauce, then ½ cup grated mozzarella cheese and 2 tablespoons grated Parmesan cheese.

Bake 15 minutes.

Makes 4 pizzas, 10 inches each

Whole Wheat Popovers

1⅓ cups milk

1½ tablespoons oil

1½ cups whole wheat pastry flour

3 eggs

*P*reheat oven to 450°F.

Combine milk, oil, and flour. Beat until smooth. Then add the eggs, one at a time, beating only until batter is smooth.

Fill well-greased muffin or popover tins three-quarters full. Bake at 450°F 15 minutes, then lower heat to 350°F and bake about 20 minutes longer.

Makes 1 dozen popovers

DESSERTS

LOW-COST DESSERTS

Millions of Americans have never even seen, let alone tasted, a dessert that didn't come in a box, an aluminum tray, or a plastic wrapper. They have missed out on some of dining's great pleasures—luscious, flavor-rich, nutritious homemade goodies that feature fresh fruits, whole grains, and delightful spices.

For many people, dessert is the most eagerly anticipated part of the meal. They *will* have it no matter how phoney the flavor, how high the cost, or how little it contributes to good health! But they can have honest ingredients that yield delectable flavors and save money at the same time. More than that, instead of serving such individuals empty calories that can be harmful to their well-being, you can provide desserts rich in nutrients that actually work to improve health.

Pies and puddings, cakes and candies, and everything between, will be better tasting and better for you when they come out of your kitchen instead of a supermarket. The economics will speak for themselves—just about any dessert sold commercially can be prepared at home at a real saving. So cut yourself from Betty Crocker's apron strings; break up with Sara Lee; go into the dessert business for yourself. Your family will bless the day!

4 large tart apples, sliced

½ cup raisins

1½ teaspoons cinnamon

1 cup corn germ

½ cup rolled oats

2 tablespoons honey

¼ cup butter, melted

Apple Crisp

Combine apples, raisins, and ½ teaspoon cinnamon. Put into a buttered 8-inch-square baking dish.

In another bowl, combine corn germ, rolled oats, and 1 teaspoon cinnamon.

Mix honey with butter, then combine with corn germ mixture. Spoon this mixture over fruit and bake at 350°F 30 minutes, or until apples are tender and topping is browned.

This crisp is excellent topped with milk or cream.

Serves 6 to 8

¼ cup bulgur

2 cups warm milk

½ cup raisins

¼ cup honey

¼ teaspoon cinnamon

3 egg yolks, beaten

3 egg whites, stiffly beaten

Bulgur-Raisin Custard

*M*ix bulgur and milk and let stand, covered, for about 1 hour. Preheat oven to 325°F. Stir raisins, honey, cinnamon, and egg yolks into bulgur mixture. Mix thoroughly, then fold in egg whites. Turn into an oiled ovenproof casserole, set casserole in a pan of hot water, and bake 1 hour and 15 minutes.

Serves 4 to 6

Carob Cupcakes

1 egg

½ cup carob powder, sifted

½ cup softened butter

1½ cups whole wheat pastry flour

½ cup sour cream, yogurt,
   or buttermilk

1 teaspoon soda

½ cup warmed honey

½ cup hot water

*P*reheat oven to 375°F.

Put ingredients into bowl in order given. Do not mix until last item has been added, then beat well. Fill greased muffin tins two-thirds full and bake 20 to 25 minutes.

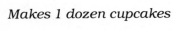

Makes 1 dozen cupcakes

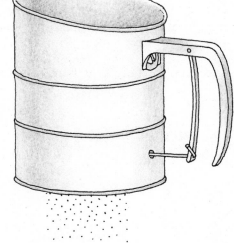

3 eggs

¾ cup oil

1 teaspoon vanilla

2 cups shredded carrots

1 cup shredded coconut

1 cup chopped walnuts

½ cup honey

1 cup raisins

1½ cups whole wheat flour

½ cup oat flour

1 teaspoon baking powder

1 teaspoon baking soda

1 teaspoon cinnamon

Carrot-Coconut Cake

*P*reheat oven to 350°F.

With electric mixer, beat eggs until light. Stir in oil, vanilla, carrots, coconut, walnuts, honey, and raisins.

Mix flours, baking powder, baking soda, and cinnamon and then add to first mixture. Do not overmix. Spread in greased 9 × 5 × 3-inch loaf pan and bake 1 hour and 10 minutes, or until done. Let stand 10 minutes and then turn out onto wire rack. Cool thoroughly, right side up.

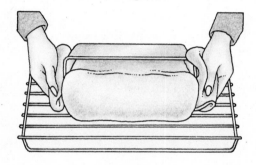

Honey-Oatmeal Cake

1 cup rolled oats

⅓ cup butter or oil

1¼ cups boiling water

½ cup honey

1 teaspoon vanilla

2 eggs

1¾ cups sifted whole wheat pastry flour

1 teaspoon baking soda

1½ teaspoons cinnamon

¼ teaspoon nutmeg

¼ teaspoon ginger (optional)

¼ cup chopped nuts

¼ cup honey

*I*n a large bowl, combine oats, butter or oil, and boiling water. Let it set 20 minutes. Add honey, vanilla, and eggs.

Preheat oven to 350°F. Add flour, baking soda, 1 teaspoon cinnamon, nutmeg, and ginger, if desired.

Grease an 8-inch-square pan with a mixture of ¼ teaspoon liquid lecithin and ¼ teaspoon oil. Pour batter into the prepared pan.

Mix nuts and ½ teaspoon cinnamon together well. Sprinkle over cake batter. Heat honey slightly and drizzle over top of cake.

Bake 30 to 40 minutes.

¾ cup skim milk powder

1 cup rolled oats

¾ cup peanut butter

½ cup honey

1 teaspoon vanilla

¼ cup toasted sesame seeds
   (toasted in 200°F oven
   20 minutes)

2 tablespoons boiling water

chopped nuts or toasted sesame
   seeds for coating balls

Peanut Butter-Sesame Balls

*M*ix skim milk powder and oats together.

In a medium-size bowl, combine peanut butter, honey, and vanilla and blend thoroughly.

Gradually add oat mixture to peanut butter mixture, blending thoroughly, using hands if necessary to mix as dough begins to stiffen. Blend in the ¼ cup of toasted sesame seeds.

Add boiling water to mixture. Blend well.

Shape into 1-inch balls. Roll in finely chopped nuts or toasted sesame seeds. For variety, roll half the mixture in chopped nuts and the other half in toasted sesame seeds.

Makes about 3 dozen balls

Index